THE COLORADO MOUNTAIN CLUB PACK GUIDE

THE

Fort Collins HIKES

JOHN GASCOYNE
and
THE FORT COLLINS GROUP
of the
COLORADO MOUNTAIN CLUB

The Colorado Mountain Club Press
Golden, Colorado

PUBLISHED BY

The Colorado Mountain Club Press
710 Tenth Street, Suite 200, Golden, Colorado 80401
303-996-2743   e-mail: cmcpress@cmc.org

Founded in 1912, The Colorado Mountain Club is the largest outdoor recreation,
education, and conservation organization in the Rocky Mountains. Look for our books
at your local bookstore or outdoor retailer or online at www.cmc.org/books.

Alan Bernhard: design, composition, and production
Dianne Nelson: copyeditor
Alan Stark: publisher

CONTACTING THE PUBLISHER

We would appreciate it if readers would alert us to any errors or
outdated information by contacting us at the address above.

DISTRIBUTED TO THE BOOK TRADE BY
Mountaineers Books, 1001 SW Klickitat Way, Suite 201, Seattle, WA
98134, 800-553-4453, www.mountaineerbooks.org

TOPOGRAPHIC MAPS are copyright 2008 and were created using
National Geographic TOPO! Outdoor Recreation software
(www.netgeomaps.com; 800-962-1643).

COVER PHOTO: Approaching the Arthur's Rock Trail from south
and east of the trailhead. Photo by Joe and Frédérique Grim.

We gratefully acknowledge the financial support of the people of
Colorado through the Scientific and Cultural Facilities District of
greater metropolitan Denver for our publishing activities.

WARNING: Although there has been an effort to make the trail descriptions in this
book as accurate as possible, some discrepancies may exist between the text and the
trails in the field. Hiking in mountainous areas is a high-risk activity. This guidebook is
not a substitute for your experience and common sense. The users of this guidebook
assume full responsibility for their own safety. Weather, terrain conditions, and indivi-
dual abilities must be considered before undertaking any of the hikes in this guide.

First Edition

ISBN 978-0-9799663-0-2

Printed in Canada

DEDICATION

The creation of this book could have been a real head banger if, as the cover suggests, I were the sole author. There were twenty trails to be hiked and carefully reported upon, natural and regional history to be researched, flora and fauna to be described, trail maps to be drafted, and a very large handful of wonderfully descriptive photographs to be taken.

The reality is that the book is a collaborative enterprise, a product of the enthusiastic and skilled efforts of the members of the Fort Collins Group of The Colorado Mountain Club. Members of the group hiked almost all of the trails; members of the group produced almost all of the maps and compelling photos. (Okay, I'm a member, too, but this is about the rest of the group.)

From the time that the book project was first described to the group, its leaders and members stepped up to the plate. The trails that were chosen for the book represent a consensus of group members' knowledge and predilections. Numerous components, such as the difficulty rating assigned to each hike, represent group input and deliberation. The editing process itself involved a good deal of back-and-forth text refining with each trail author.

If errors are found in this pack guide, as the editor and final filter, I accept full responsibility. If you find this book useful and commendable, as you most likely will, then join me in giving credit and kudos to the Fort Collins Group of The Colorado Mountain Club.

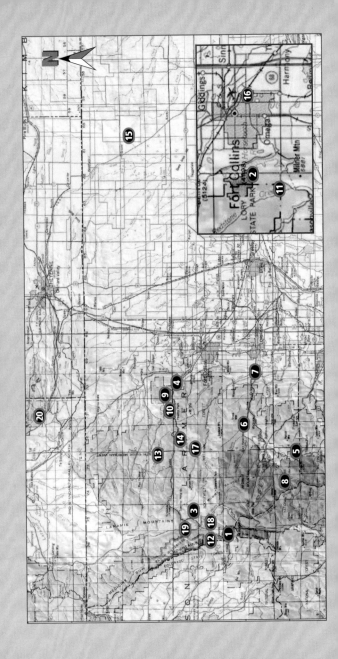

CONTENTS

Acknowledgments 6

Foreword 7

Introduction... 9

The Ten Essential Systems 11

THE HIKES

1. American Lakes (or Michigan Lakes) 14
2. Arthur's Rock.................................. 18
3. Big South..................................... 22
4. Black Powder Trail 26
5. Chasm Lake 30
6. Crosier Mountain 34
7. Devil's Backbone—Wild Loop Trail 38
8. Flattop Mountain and Hallett Peak 42
9. Greyrock Trail 46
10. Hewlett Gulch 50
11. Horsetooth Rock............................... 54
12. Montgomery Pass (#986) 58
13. Mount Margaret 62
14. Mount McConnell.............................. 66
15. Pawnee Buttes 70
16. Poudre Trail 74
17. Stormy Peaks Trail to Stormy Peaks Pass........ 78
18. Trap Park 82
19. Twin Crater Lakes............................. 86
20. Vedauwoo/Turtle Rock Loop................... 90

Youngsters in the Woods............................. 94

About the Author 95

Checklist... 96

ACKNOWLEDGMENTS

This is the part where I thank Ms. Dobbs, my fourth-grade English teacher who drubbed me mercilessly into an appreciation of the language; my great-grandfather for siring my grandfather—that sort of lengthy tribute. Forget all that. In no particular order whatsoever, I want to acknowledge and offer deep gratitude to: Paul Weber, chair of the Fort Collins Group of The Colorado Mountain Club; Jeff Eisele, group member and project supporter from the beginning; all of the wonderfully supportive members of the Fort Collins Group, most particularly those whose names appear as authors and photographers in the book; Alan Stark, CMC Press Publisher and constant guide throughout this effort; Dianne Nelson for her reasoned and reasonable copyediting; Alan Bernhard of Boulder Bookworks, a classical book designer with a feel for the outdoors; Alan Apt, outdoor adventurer and snowshoeing expert, who introduced me to this project; Ward Luthi, whose vast knowledge of hiking and the wilds has been a large part of my education; David Bye, for providing years of clarity in a fuzzy world; Bear Gebhardt, extraordinary writer and writing compadre for forty years or more; and esteemed hiking and, talkin'-as-we're-walkin', problem-solving companions over the past many years, Shawn Bowman, Alan Budreau, Marti Foxhoven, Mims Harris, Bob Martino, and Robin Nielsen. Finally, a special thanks to Xander Bowman, age seven, and Lucy Bowman, age five, for showing me, over and over, how to see nature through eyes of youthful wonder.

Foreword

The Fort Collins Group of The Colorado Mountain Club invites you to experience the majesty of Colorado's mountains and plains. The northern Front Range of Colorado spans a series of diverse ecological zones, from arid high plains to alpine tundra, interspersed with scenic rivers and burbling streams along the way.

From high peaks to broad plains, our members have selected a sampling of their favorite hiking trails for inclusion in this guidebook. Inside you will find a trail just right for you. Wildflowers are abundant on many trails from late spring to midsummer. Elk, moose, deer, turkey, and grouse are only a few of the wildlife species you may see along the way.

The Colorado Mountain Club urges you to follow safety guidelines when hiking. Mountain terrain and weather are unforgiving. Be sure to carry essential items you need to survive in case of unexpected circumstances. Be alert to Colorado's changing weather; always carry extra clothing and rain gear. Be aware of your surroundings and view wildlife from a safe distance. Tell someone where you are going and when you expect to return. Even better, hike with a friend or the CMC—guests are welcome on many hikes.

Help us protect the fragile environment of this unique area by practicing Leave No Trace principles. Always keep pets on a leash. Do not shortcut trails. Pack out what you pack in. Take only photos; leave only footprints.

Enjoy and be safe.

PAUL WEBER, Chairperson
Fort Collins Group
The Colorado Mountain Club

Footbridge on Greyrock Trail.

BEST FORT COLLINS HIKES

Introduction

Whether you're a relative newcomer, or have been around since the river rocks had square edges, you probably have a good notion of the wonderful hiking opportunities available in this area. Allow *The Best Fort Collins Hikes* to be your ticket to twenty superb outdoor adventures, all close by or readily accessible from Fort Collins.

There were a number of considerations and objectives in the selection of hikes and drafting of the book:

- Variety of experiences—from the unique and sandy beauty of the Pawnee Buttes to the alpine majesty of Chasm Lake, the guide offers a full palette of exciting hikes. We even crossed the state line to include Vedauwoo, a Wyoming site favored by many Fort Collins hikers.

- Degrees of difficulty—the book moves from the ease of the flat and paved Poudre Trail to the rigors of the Flattop Mountain and Hallett Peak hike and provides many options in between.

- Year-round hiking—most of the described trails provide four-season opportunities; a few of them require patience until spring sunshine wears down a heavy winter snowpack.

- Listing of the hikes—after considering other possibilities, we decided to list the hikes alphabetically. This, hopefully, will encourage readers to browse the entire book, looking for the one hike that will be most rewarding on a given day.

We are daily visited with evidence of the fragility of our unique planet and its intricate and mutually dependent systems. As we enjoy the hikes and adventures described in this book, we can adopt a line from the medical doctor's playbook: "First, do no harm." In the woods, this can include staying on the trail, leaving wildlife alone, and packing out whatever we

Wildflowers brighten the hike across Stormy Peak Pass.   PHOTO BY JEFF EISELE

pack in. Whenever possible, we can bike or carpool to the trailhead. Each of us can become a vocal advocate for preserving the extraordinary gift that is the Colorado outdoors.

Some months ago, I helped chaperon some junior high school students on a hike on the Cub Lake Trail in Rocky Mountain National Park. We were graced with the appearance of some curious marmots and a sizable elk herd. While the young people were enthusiastic and eager to learn, it was apparent that many or most of them had spent little time in an outdoors environment. The healthy future of the wilder places will be won or lost by younger generations. We can invest in that future by helping young folks explore the wonder and the worth of our natural heritage.

The Colorado Mountain Club has been around since 1912. It is about more than hiking and mountain climbing—CMC is a major conservation force in the Rocky Mountains. If you are not yet a member, consider joining. As you expand your hiking opportunities, you will be supporting the organization's extraordinary preservation efforts. More information is available at www.cmc.org.

The Ten Essential Systems

This pack guide has been prepared by members of the Fort Collins Chapter of The Colorado Mountain Club and published by The Colorado Mountain Club Press. Distribution and use of the guide are intended for the general public as well as for CMC members. If you are not already familiar with the Ten Essential Systems, take a few minutes to study the following information and, most importantly, incorporate the systems into all of your hiking activities.

1. **Hydration.** Carry at least two liters or quarts of water on any hike. For a longer hike, consider a water purification system. If you don't drink until you are thirsty, you have waited too long.

2. **Nutrition.** Eat a good breakfast before your hike; pack a healthy lunch—fruits, vegetables, carbs, etc.—and carry some trail mix and/or a couple of nutrition bars.

3. **Sun protection.** Include sunglasses, a large-brimmed hat, lip balm, and sunscreen with an SPF rating of 45 or higher.

4. **Insulation (extra clothing).** Colorado weather can change in an instant, so you want to be prepared. At all times, carry a rain/wind parka and pants, extra layers of outer clothing, wool or synthetic insulating inner layers, gloves or mittens, a warm hat, and socks. Cotton clothing retains moisture and does not insulate when it is damp—including from perspiration—so it should not be part of your hiking gear.

5. **Navigation.** Carry a map of your hiking area and a reliable (non-Cracker Jack) compass. A GPS unit can add to your ability to navigate; it is not a substitute for the map and compass.

6. **Illumination.** Include a headlamp or flashlight and extra batteries. A headlamp is probably the better

choice—you can keep both hands free while you work or hike. (Hiking in the darkness is not recommended if it can be avoided.)

7. **First-aid supplies.** Include Ace bandages, a bandana, duct tape (usable as a Band-Aid or for blister protection), moleskin for blisters, toilet paper, and a Ziploc bag for used toilet paper. Consider carrying a small bottle of alcohol and/or hydrogen peroxide as a germicide when dealing with small abrasions or cuts. A snakebite kit, while seldom needed, could round out your supplies.

8. **Fire.** Be sure to have waterproof matches, a lighter, fire ribbon, or other commercial fire starter, and make certain that all of these will work in wet, cold, and windy conditions. Cotton dryer lint, steel wool, hardened tree sap, and dry pine needles can all serve as kindling.

9. **Repair kit and tools.** A pocketknife, emergency whistle, signal mirror, and low-temperature electrician's or duct tape are handy for all types of repairs.

10. **Emergency shelter.** Carry a space blanket and parachute or other nylon cord or a bivouac sack. Large plastic leaf bags are handy for emergency rain gear, pack covers, and survival shelters.

Depending on the length of the trip and the season, you may also want to include:

- A foam pad for sitting or sleeping on.
- A metal cup and a gas stove so that you can melt snow (trying to eat snow as a water source is not recommended).
- A snow shovel (a Frisbee or metal dish can be an emergency substitute).
- If you have had trouble with knees or ankles, carry a neoprene brace in your day pack—also a good cushion when eating lunch while balancing on a granite slab.

A beautiful day on Montgomery Pass.

PHOTO BY JOE GRIM

- Walking sticks—the better ones are spring-loaded and have canted handles. Walking sticks can take a great deal of weight off of your knees and legs while hiking and, at the same time, provide some upper-body workout. Practice planting the tips quietly to avoid annoying your hiking companions and putting forest creatures to flight.

This information is intended as a starting place in your preparations for hiking in Colorado; it does not tell you everything that you need to know in the woods or how to deal with all emergencies. There are many programs and publications that can increase your knowledge base. Please visit The Colorado Mountain Club's website at www.cmc.org for more information.

1. American Lakes
(or Michigan Lakes)

BY DON CARPENTER

MAPS	Trails Illustrated, Poudre River/Cameron Pass, Number 112 Trails Illustrated, Rocky Mountain National Park, Number 200
ELEVATION GAIN	1,400 feet to the lower lake
RATING	Difficult
ROUND-TRIP DISTANCE	7.3 miles
ROUND-TRIP TIME	4–5 hours
NEAREST LANDMARK	Cameron Pass

COMMENT: This trail provides easy access to a high, wide alpine meadow experience. It travels through Colorado State Park State Forest, on the western side of the Continental Divide. The trail begins on an old logging road and climbs through evergreens and past small, snow-fed, swollen streams. To the north are views of the Diamond Peaks in the Medicine Bow Range, which extends into Wyoming. The Never Summer Range is seen to the east and south. The American Lakes, sometimes called Michigan Lakes on older maps, comprise two easily accessible lakes. A third lake, Snow Lake, involves a rocky scramble.

Depending on spring temperatures, the trail may not be easily navigable until late June or July. The Nohku Crags (from the Arapahoe *hoh'onookee*, meaning "Eagle Rocks") form the western boundary above the lakes and shade the lakes from the late afternoon sun. As you enjoy the panoramic views of peaks and tundra, look for wildflowers like the glacier lily in late June. Other Never Summer Range views on this hike include Static Peak, with Mount Richthofen in the background, and Lulu Mountain and Thunder Mountain, all part of the Continental Divide bordering on Rocky Mountain National Park.

The Nokhu Crags, a highlight of the American Lakes hike.

PHOTO BY DON CARPENTER

GETTING THERE: Take U.S. 287 north from Fort Collins to the junction of Colorado 14 at Ted's Place. Turn left (west) and proceed 62.7 miles up the Poudre Canyon to the turnoff for the trailhead. The turnoff is 2.6 miles west of Cameron Pass on the left (south), side of the road and is marked by a sign for the Crags and Lake Agnes. Continue 1.5 miles to the trailhead, following the signs for American Lakes and staying left past the Lake Agnes trailhead. A parking area is at the end of the road. A state park fee or sticker is required. Alternately, you can park at Cameron Pass, cross Colorado 14 to the south side, and follow the Michigan Ditch service road until the trail crosses the ditch and leads to the American Lakes. (Michigan Ditch collects water on the western side of the Continental Divide and diverts it to the eastern plains.)

THE ROUTE: Starting at the east end of the parking lot, follow the old logging road along the Michigan River for 1.42 miles, then cross the service road for the Michigan Ditch. Continue on the other side of the ditch, following the Michigan River on the

Looking toward Mount Richtofen, on left, and Static Peak.

PHOTO BY DON CARPENTER

east side of a valley, then cross the river on a wooden foot-bridge at 2.8 miles. Watch for wildlife, especially moose feasting on the river willows in the valley beyond the footbridge. The trail then goes through a series of switchbacks until it finally emerges from the trees. Enjoy alpine vistas of the Never Summer Range as you continue to the rock crossing at the east outlet of the lakes. (An older trail parallels the Michigan River to the lakes but is not the preferred route.) Go along the lower lake on either the north or south side to the second lake.

Time and weather permitting, you may also wish to make side trips to Thunder Pass (0.8 mile from the rock crossing and a 106-foot elevation gain), easily visible to the east along the marked trail, or on to Snow Lake. The scramble to Snow Lake is 0.5 mile farther from the rock crossing.

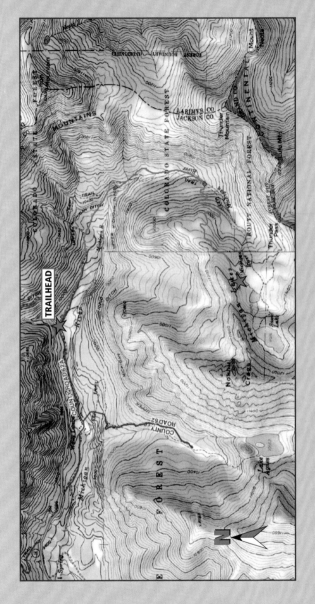

TRAILHEAD

AMERICAN LAKES (or Michigan Lakes)

2. Arthur's Rock

BY ERIC ERSLEV

MAPS	USGS, Horsetooth Reservoir, 7.5 minute Lory State Park trail map
ELEVATION GAIN	1,150 feet
RATING	Moderate
ROUND-TRIP DISTANCE	3.4 miles
ROUND-TRIP TIME	3 hours
NEAREST LANDMARK	LaPorte

COMMENT: Arthur's Rock Trail is the most popular hike at Lory State Park. It features an easily accessible route through shaded valleys filled with wild plums, upland meadows, ponderosa pine groves, and bare granitic knobs. Along with Horsetooth Rock to the south, the craggy summit of Arthur's Rock provides the best views of Fort Collins and the intervening, sinuous hogbacks and 6-mile-long Horsetooth Reservoir. The hike provides a great place to visualize the uplift of the Rocky Mountains 60 million years ago as it tilted the strata to the east and transformed a shallow sea into a mountain belt.

Interest points along the way: (1) the narrow gulch just beyond the trailhead formed by a transition from nonresistant, 300-million-year-old sandstone to hard, 1.4-billion-year-old granitic rocks; (2) open meadows and ponderosa pine forests on friable schist below Arthur's Rock; and (3) the bare summits and cliffs of Arthur's Rocks, formed by a large intrusion of 1.4-billion-year-old granitic rock.

GETTING THERE: From Fort Collins, take U.S. 287 north to Colorado 14, (County Road 54G), through LaPorte, and turn left (west) on to County Road 52E (just past Vern's Place); drive to Bellvue. Turn left at the Bellvue Grange (County Road 23N), and go south 1.4 miles to County Road 25G. Turn right and go 1.6 miles to the entrance of Lory State Park. Purchase a day pass or season pass at the ranger station, and drive south to the end of the road.

Native grasses along the way to Arthur's Rock.   PHOTO BY ERIC ERSLEV

THE ROUTE: Arthur's Rock trailhead is immediately west of the parking lot, just beyond an interpretive kiosk and restrooms. The well-maintained, hiking-only trail quickly leaves the NNW–trending valley, formed by erosion of the Pennsylvanian Fountain Formation sandstone, and enters Arthur's Gulch, which cuts through the more resistant, 1.4-billion-year-old granitic rocks. This narrow valley shelters thick vegetation, including wild plums; in the warmer months, it is a good place to be alert for bull snakes and rattlesnakes.

Switchbacks up the south side of the gulch offer a preview of narrow hillside sections to come. First, however, the trail enters a pleasing area of grassy upland meadows, interspersed with younger ponderosa pines, chokecherries, and cottonwood

The final scramble to the top.

PHOTO BY ERIC ERSLEV

trees. The grasses give way to mature ponderosa pines, and the trail begins ascending more switchbacks up the north side of the valley toward the rocky exposures of Arthur's Rock itself. Just below the first outcrops, 1.1 miles along, a grove of ponderosa pines offers shelter from the sun; an adjacent rocky vantage point provides an excellent mid-hike spot for a break and a view to the east. The trail continues upward, following the contact between easily eroded, mica-rich schist and the coarse-grained quartz- and feldspar-rich granitic intrusive that forms Arthur's Rock. Pines shelter the top of the valley as the trail climbs toward a saddle at the intersection with the Timber Trail. At this point, begin a short scramble up a rocky gully to reach the bare rock knobs that form the summit points of Arthur's Rock. The west summit is the highest, but each summit provides a different view of Fort Collins, the foothills, and Horsetooth Reservoir.

TRAILHEAD

3. Big South

TEXT BY EILEEN EDELMAN
PHOTOS BY PAMELA CRAIG

MAPS	Trails Illustrated, Poudre River/Cameron Pass, Number 112
ELEVATION GAIN	800 feet
RATING	Easy to moderate
ROUND-TRIP DISTANCE	6 miles, up to 14 possible
ROUND-TRIP TIME	4 hours
NEAREST LANDMARK	Mile marker 75, Colorado 14

COMMENT: This hike follows the Cache La Poudre River upstream from Poudre Canyon south to Grass Creek, at mile 3, and then on to a washed-out bridge at about mile 7. Parts of the trail are lovely flat strolls on pine needles at river level; other sections climb high on the wall of the magnificent gorge formed by the river. Some spectacular sections of the trail cross large talus slopes below the gorge walls. You will enjoy the big, open rock traverses, river views, wildflowers, and luxurious forest scenery.

GETTING THERE: From Fort Collins, take U.S. 287 to Colorado 14 at Ted's Place. Turn left (west) and drive 48.7 miles, just past mile marker 75. The trailhead parking lot is on the left, just before the highway crosses a bridge. Restroom facilities are available at the campground, just beyond the bridge.

THE ROUTE: The beginning of the trail is lined with green gentian, also called monument plant. This rare plant appears as clumps of basal leaves with reddish stems when it is young, and as a tall, green-flowered, elaborate structure years later when it blooms. Continue through aspen and evergreen groves. Wonderful river scenery will be on your right, and lovely forest views will be to the left. In about fifteen minutes of moderate hiking, you will enter the Comanche Peak Wilderness Area. Look for the talus slopes on your left; they will increase in size and height as you continue walking.

Along the Big South Fork of the Poudre River.

PHOTO BY PAMELA CRAIG

The U.S. Forest Service has designated the Big South corridor as a Travel Zone, which means that camping is permitted only in designated sites. You will pass the first of these in another twenty minutes. Just beyond this campsite is the first of the open rock traverses. Stop here for a break, even just to take a picture. There are very few long, open views along this trail, but there are wonderful views up- and downstream from the rock-traverse sections. The trail is well built here, and the footing is excellent.

The second long, open traverse is just beyond campsite 5. This one is lined with wild roses, usually in flower by late June. The trail soon drops to the level of the river and a perfect picnic spot: a large boulder wall and a tree with gnarled roots provide a natural bench for several hikers. You will soon be hiking away from the river until the trail crosses a bridge over beautiful May Creek, about 2.3 miles from the trailhead. Continue for a half hour more to the top of another rock

A view worth hiking to.

PHOTO BY PAMELA CRAIG

traverse. A large, open area is located here with views
upstream and lots of large rocks for seating. This traverse then
drops rather steeply to the point where Grass Creek comes in
from the left. This is the turnaround point for a 6-mile hike.

The trail continues another 4 miles from the Grass Creek
crossing to the washed-out bridge, again alternating easy-
walking streamside sections with climbing rather steeply up
and down the walls of the gorge. The scenery is beautiful
throughout; the most dramatic views are in the first 3 miles.

SIDEBAR: A SNOWSHOE ROUTE, TOO.

In winter, Big South is an excellent snowshoe trail. By early
February, there should be more than enough snow to cover the
rocks, and the snow lasts through early April. Against the
snow, the aspen trunks that look so white in summer appear
to be gold or pale green. The snow will also reveal abundant
animal tracks in the open areas along the river.

TRAILHEAD

Big South
Campground

4. Black Powder Trail

BY JOHN GASCOYNE

MAPS	USGS, LaPorte, 7.5 minute
ELEVATION GAIN	500 feet
RATING	Easy to moderate
ROUND-TRIP DISTANCE	1.5 miles
ROUND-TRIP TIME	1.5–2 hours
NEAREST LANDMARK	Ted's Place, at the junction of U.S. 287 and Colorado 14

COMMENT: The Black Powder Trail begins in Gateway Park, located at the confluence of the Poudre River and the North Fork of the Poudre and is the site of the former Fort Collins water treatment plant that opened in 1903. During the Depression, Civilian Conservation Corps (CCC) workers built roads and trails in the park area. In 2004, the Picnic Rock Fire raged through much of the park. We can witness here how a natural area restores itself after a burning. In 2006, the Fort Collins Naturals Areas program began administering the park and renamed it Gateway Natural Area. Because of its natural beauty and closeness to the city, it is a popular destination—a nice hike that can be accomplished in a half day, including driving time.

Gateway Park is an inviting place, with large, grassy areas, picnic pavilions, barbecue grills, and clean restrooms. As with other mountain areas, rattlesnakes are occasionally encountered, so exercise normal caution. The park is a fee area—four dollars for passenger cars and eight dollars for vans. Hours of use are 7 a.m. to 9 p.m. from Memorial Day to Labor Day and from 8 a.m. to sunset the rest of the year.

The expression "all over the board" springs to mind as efforts are made to assess the difficulty of the Black Powder Trail. The consensus of a CMC focus group was: "easy" because it is a short distance, and "moderate" because of the elevation-gaining switchbacks. The city's website lists the trail as

The North Fork of the Poudre River at Gateway Park.

PHOTO BY JOHN GASCOYNE

"moderate to difficult." So, if you've been looking for an "easy–moderate–difficult" hike, you've arrived. Lace up your tennies and start chugging along.

GETTING THERE: From downtown Fort Collins, take U.S. 287 about 10 miles to Ted's Place, which marks the junction with Colorado 14. Turn left (west) and go 5.3 miles on Colorado 14 to the park entrance on your right.

THE ROUTE: From the parking area, walk across the park in a northeasterly direction and cross the footbridge over the river. Stay on the dirt road for a short distance to the sign indicating the trailhead on the right. The lower portion of the trail affords a good opportunity for aerobic exercise, as it is somewhat steep. It is, nonetheless, within the capability of most hikers. You will soon come to signage that offers a choice between staying on the trail, to the left, or going to the right to a scenic overlook. It is worth taking a few minutes to follow the short path to the overlook. There is mild exposure on this portion, so careful walking is advised. This detour also holds a

CCC stairways on the Black Powder Trail.

PHOTO BY JOHN GASCOYNE

wonderful example of CCC labor—a granite staircase artfully built into the trail.

Retrace your steps to the sign and continue walking up the hill and through the trees. The trail will begin to flatten out as you approach the terminus. In the proper season on this stretch, you will be treated to a kaleidoscope of wildflowers sprinkled among knee-high native grasses. Close to the top, you will come to an unmarked fork in the trail. Stay to the left for the more direct and easier path to the terminus of the trail. At the top, you will enjoy a panoramic view that includes Colorado 14 snaking through Poudre Canyon and, looking northeasterly, Seaman Reservoir and dam.

When you start back from the top, you can retrace your steps or, if you want a slightly more challenging route, follow the less-distinct portion of the trail that goes west for just a few paces and then curves around to the north. This will circle around to the fork in the trail and put you back on the main path for the trip down.

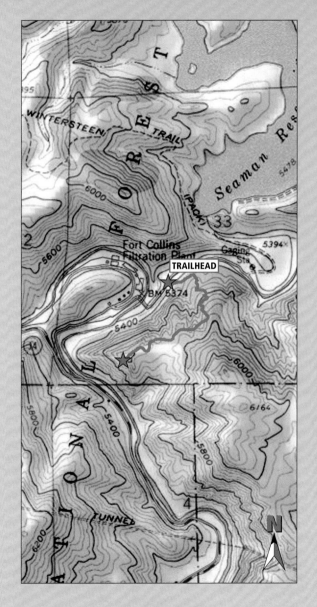

5. Chasm Lake

BY SANDY JORDAN

MAPS	Trails Illustrated, Rocky Mountain National Park. Number 112
ELEVATION GAIN	2,355 feet
RATING	Moderate
ROUND-TRIP DISTANCE	8.4 miles
ROUND-TRIP TIME	4–5 hours
NEAREST LANDMARK	Estes Park

COMMENT: The Chasm Lake Trail provides a classic above-tree-line adventure. You will enjoy alternating views of Longs Peak, Mount Meeker, Mount Lady Washington, Twin Sisters, and Estes Cone. The trail begins below treeline as it winds through a spruce forest, then opens into an alpine meadow. Next, it traverses through an alpine wetland, complete with waterfalls, to finally summit at the tarn known as Chasm Lake. Hikers are treated to the comical antics of the marmot population, while ground squirrels, pikas, ptarmigans, and various songbirds are almost-guaranteed wildlife sightings. On occasion, you may share the trail with a pair of llamas, as the park rangers use these sturdy pack animals to restock.

GETTING THERE: From downtown Estes Park, go east on U.S. 36 and quickly turn on Colorado 7, heading south. When you come to mile marker 9, the Longs Peak trailhead road, turn right and follow the road to the trailhead parking lot. On a given day, this lot fills up quickly and you may see cars parked along the road approaching the parking area. Park officials seem to tolerate off-road parking at this trailhead. Just beyond the ranger station, at the trailhead, is a sign-in book requesting that hikers sign in and sign back out.

THE ROUTE: The trail to Chasm Lake follows the Longs Peak Trail for the first 3.5 miles. This part of the trail follows a moderate incline over a nicely maintained footpath. About an hour out

A golden reflection on Chasm Lake.   PHOTO BY TODD CAUDLE

from the trailhead, a sign indicates the beginning of the tundra region. Here the trail begins to open up, and it is soon completely above treeline. Another sign, 1.7 miles from Chasm Lake, introduces a beautifully constructed stone stairway that facilitates your elevation gain through the alpine tundra. The trail turns south in front of Mount Lady Washington and, about 2.5 hours from the trailhead, you will see a privy and the spur trail to Chasm Lake. Although the spur trail is only 0.7 mile long, it takes about half an hour to trek along the edge of a beautiful gorge and through a scenic wetland. Snow on this portion of the trail often remains through the middle of July.

A second privy and a National Park Service patrol cabin mark the beginning of a fifteen-minute rock scramble up to Chasm Lake. No defined trail is present here, but multiple rock cairns indicate the general direction to the lake. Hikers who stop short of the scramble are treated to breathtaking views of the waterfalls and of the profuse wildflowers of the alpine

On the trail to Chasm Lake.   PHOTO BY SANDY JORDAN

wetland and the surrounding mountains. It is even more awe inspiring if you reach the lake. The view of the Diamond Face from the southwest corner of the lake is represented on the Colorado quarter. Consider if it is worth the extra effort to be able to hold up a quarter and tell your flatland friends that you've been there.

This hike should be undertaken only after July 1, unless you're prepared to traverse steep, narrow portions of the trail, burdened with substantial snow cover. It is highly advisable to begin your hike before 8 a.m., as summer thunderstorms are quite common after the noon hour and can be particularly dangerous above treeline. A moderate pace will take you to the lake before noon. Linger at the lake just long enough for a brief rest, a short snack, and a deep inhalation of the mountain views. Pacing yourself this way, you can scurry down the trail to treeline and stay ahead of most storms.

TRAILHEAD

6. Crosier Mountain

BY STEVE MARTIN

MAPS	Trails Illustrated, Cache La Poudre/ Big Thompson, Number 101 USGS, Glen Haven 7.5 minute
ELEVATION GAIN	Glen Haven Trail (931W): 2,485 feet Rainbow Trail (1013): 2,675 feet Garden Gate Trail (931E): 3,250 feet
ROUND-TRIP DISTANCE	Glen Haven Trail (931W): 8.4 miles Rainbow Trail (1013): 7.5 miles Garden Gate Trail (931E): 9.9 miles
ROUND-TRIP TIME	Glen Haven Trail (931W): 5–8 hours Rainbow Trail (1013): 5–8 hours Garden Gate Trail (931E): 6–10 hours
RATING	Three trails: moderate to difficult
NEAREST LANDMARK	Drake

COMMENT: Crosier Mountain provides a variety of hikes along three well-maintained trails that have differing elevation gains and views. The three share a steep, final, 0.5-mile spur trail to the summit, a point that offers superb vistas of Rocky Mountain National Park's high peaks. When the snow is deep, route finding can be difficult on Garden Gate Trail (931E). In August 2007, nine challenging geocaches for the keen hiker/geocacher were accessible by Crosier's trail system. Be sure to find the benchmark at the summit. Four separate "ranked peaks" form Crosier's bulk—take some time to discover them on your map and consider hiking all of them off trail once you've whetted your appetite on the marvelous trails to the main Crosier summit.

GETTING THERE: Take U.S. 34 west from Loveland about 17 miles to Drake; turn right on County Road 43 (Devil's Gulch Road) toward Glen Haven for 2.2 miles to the Garden Gate trailhead, on the left. Go 5.5 miles from Drake to reach the Rainbow trailhead on the left. The Glen Haven trailhead is at 7.3 miles, just past the horse stable at the upper end of the town of Glen

The three trails feature geologic formations framing
distant panoramas.   PHOTO BY STEVE MARTIN

Haven. All trailheads are well signed, but the trail display at
Garden Gate isn't very visible from the small parking area. To
access this trail, go through the small gate and up a short hill
to the official information area.

THE ROUTES:

Glen Haven Trail: Head up the dirt road as it switchbacks
up the initial steep terrain; the road becomes a trail and, after
about 1.5 miles, you'll arrive at Piper Meadows. This is a great
spot for a picnic and a turnaround point for a short hike. See if
you can find the foundations of Harry Piper's old farm
buildings. At about an 8,000-foot elevation, ascend more
switchbacks. Signage for the junction of Trails 931 and 1013 is
about 2.5 miles along the trail. From here, gradually climb
about 1.5 miles through lodgepole pine forests to a sign, where
you'll turn right to the marvelous summit views. The final 0.5
mile is the steepest part of your hike, but the trail is enjoyable.

Portions of the trails take you through aspen groves.

PHOTO BY STEVE MARTIN

Rainbow Trail: Hike up moderately steep terrain to a meadow at 7,600 feet and enjoy splendid views to the north and east. After 1.75 miles, you will reach Trail 931 from Glen Haven; follow it to the summit. Try to locate the old Malmberg cabin hidden below you in the trees, just southeast of the trail junction. It was built more than 100 years ago.

Garden Gate Trail: Beautiful switchbacks make the intimidating steepness of the first mile easy, and you quickly reach a large meadow that's a great location for a rest, a picnic, or a turn-back if you desire a relatively short outing. If you go farther, you will go over a saddle for a first sighting of Crosier's summit. From there, descend into True Gulch and follow the trail as it switchbacks sharply up to a sparsely treed ridge that offers spectacular views of the mountains to the south and west. After you've hiked 4.5 miles, the trail joins the Glen Haven Trail. Turn left here for the final 0.5 mile to the top.

TRAILHEAD

TRAILHEAD

TRAILHEAD

CROSIER MOUNTAIN 37

7. Devil's Backbone— ✓
Wild Loop Trail

BY LARRY AND DARIA MOSKOWITZ

MAPS	Larimer County Parks map
ELEVATION GAIN	225 feet
RATING	Easy
ROUND-TRIP DISTANCE	2.5 miles
ROUND-TRIP TIME	1–1.5 hours
NEAREST LANDMARK	Loveland

COMMENT: The Devil's Backbone is a unique rock formation perched atop the hogback in the foothills west of Loveland. A short and easy hike provides panoramic views of the grasslands and mountains to the west, all seen from a unique geologic showcase. Within the Devil's Backbone Open Space, beyond the Backbone itself, is an extensive trail system that allows options for much longer hikes.

The trail described here, the Wild Loop, is an easy 2.5-mile interpretive hike. It is named for Alfred Wild, who purchased the southern part of the backbone in the late nineteenth century. The Louden Ditch runs through the area near the trailhead, and excavations for gypsum, found in abundance here, can be seen around the first part of the trail.

The Backbone itself, which runs from the northwest to the southeast for about 3.5 miles, is composed primarily of Dakota sandstone. The hogback was formed from layers of sedimentary rock that were laid down in stratified layers, then tilted at an angle and eroded at different rates. The five different formations that comprise the hogback are: the Lykins, around 245 million years ago, and the Jelm formation, about 230 million years ago, both of which are from the early Triassic Period; the Entrada Sandstone, 208 million years ago, and the gray Morrison formation, 160 million years ago, from the early and late Jurassic Period, respectively; and the gray-

Devil's Backbone is known for unique rock formations.

brown to tan sandstone Dakota Group, 120 million years ago, from the early to middle Cretaceous Period. The hogbacks were produced by the same forces that created the Rocky Mountains (the Laramide Orogeny) around 60 million years ago. These layers were pushed up into folds that later eroded into what we see today.

The Devil's Backbone Open Space is open year-round, but for day use only. Rock climbing is prohibited and dogs must be on leash. There are restrooms at the trailhead.

GETTING THERE: From the intersection of U.S. 287 and U.S. 34 (Eisenhower Boulevard) in Loveland, drive west 4 miles on Eisenhower. The turnoff to the trailhead parking is on the right side of the road. Look for signs to Devil's Backbone Open Space and Hidden Valley Estates.

Exciting views highlight the hike. PHOTO BY LARRY AND DARIA MOSKOWITZ

THE ROUTE: From the trailhead, the Wild Loop Trail goes 0.4 mile
and splits into an upper section, for hikers only, and a lower,
multi-use section that accommodates hikers, bikers, and
horses. The upper section, which goes closer to the Backbone,
is 0.9 mile long, and the lower section is 0.8 mile. As the route
climbs closer to the Backbone, rock outcroppings of different
color and origin are exposed and can be seen in and along the
trail. The trail climbs gently to the overlook and to a short
loop going directly to the Keyhole and the vistas framed by
this unique bit of geology. From March 1 to June 15, the trail
to the Keyhole is closed to protect raven nesting sites. The
high rock formations of the Backbone provide excellent habi-
tat for raptors and other birds. White streaks on the rocks
indicate nesting areas and perching spots.

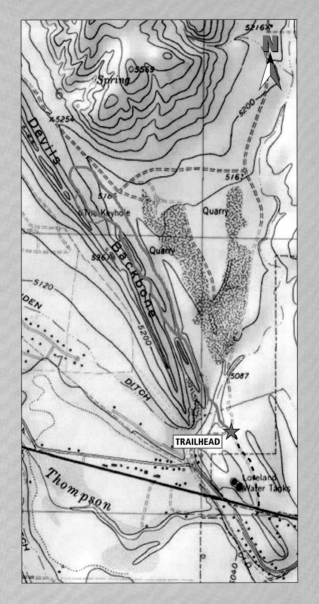

TRAILHEAD

Spring

Devils

Backbone

The Keyhole

Quarry

Quarry

DITCH

Thompson

Loveland
Water Tanks

8. Flattop Mountain and Hallett Peak

BY TINA GABLE

MAPS	Trails Illustrated, Rocky Mountain National Park, Number 200 Trails Illustrated, Longs Peak, Number 301
ELEVATION GAIN	Flattop: 2,849 feet Hallett Peak: 3,238 feet
RATING	Difficult
ROUND-TRIP DISTANCE	10 miles
ROUND-TRIP TIME	5–6 hours
NEAREST LANDMARK	Estes Park

COMMENT: The hike up Flattop Mountain and Hallett Peak is truly a memorable experience. The switchbacks up the eastern slope of Flattop, and the last few hundred feet of rock scrambling to Hallett's summit, may be daunting for those unaccustomed to long uphill or higher-elevation hikes, but this is a well-marked trail with no technical or exposed hiking. Wildlife sightings are possible as the trail progresses up Flattop's eastern flank to the Continental Divide and one of the park's most prominently visible landmarks, Hallett Peak. Start this hike early in order to secure a parking spot at the trailhead and to avoid possible afternoon thunderstorms.

GETTING THERE: From Loveland, take U.S. 34 to Estes Park. Turn left on Moraine Avenue (U.S. 36), and continue to the Beaver Meadow entrance station of Rocky Mountain National Park. Go west about 0.2 mile to Bear Lake Road. Turn left and follow Bear Lake Road 9 miles to the Bear Lake parking lot.

THE ROUTE: Bear Lake and the Flattop Mountain trailhead are located a short jaunt west from the parking lot. The summit of Hallett Peak is out of view at the beginning of your hike. Before seeing the actual summit, you will be looking at its

Hallett Peak, with Flattop Mountain to the right.   PHOTO BY TINA GABLE

sheer northern face and the wedge-shaped "false peak." To the
north of Hallett are Tyndall Gorge and the massive hulk of
Flattop Mountain. The trail to Flattop is the park's primary
access to the Continental Divide, as well the route to summit
Hallett Peak.

From the eastern shore of Bear Lake, head north through
the aspen grove and pine forest for 0.5 mile. Turn left at the
marked Flattop/Bierstadt junction and continue up the

modest grade. Intermittent gaps in the trees allow views of Glacier Gorge and the imposing western flank of Longs Peak and Keyboard of the Winds.

The trail continues to wind through pine forest for another 0.5 mile to the Flattop/Fern-Odessa junction. Turn left here to continue up the Flattop Mountain Trail. Dream Lake Overlook, at 10,500 feet, offers a nice chance to rest.

Emerald Lake Overlook, at 11,300 feet, is another rest stop and provides the opportunity for some exciting photographs. Tyndall Gorge, below, and Hallett's heavily striated north face dominate this view. The summit of Hallett's Peak is clearly visible at this point, appearing as a rounded hump, approximately 400 feet higher and 0.4 mile further west than the "false peak" that you saw from Bear Lake. The next 1.5 miles will steepen in parts, making this a more difficult section. This is a good time to drink lots of water and to take rest stops while you enjoy the striking scenery.

The last 0.25 mile starts to level out as you approach Flattop's summit. Once you are on top, the actual summit is difficult to identify, and repeat hikers no longer look for the exact highest point. You are now standing on the Continental Divide as the expanse of Bighorn Flats stretches out in front of you. To the west, you will see Grand Lake, Shadow Mountain Lake, and Lake Granby.

From the summit to the top of Hallett is another 0.5 mile and a 389-foot elevation gain. This part of the trail is considered unimproved, but the way is clearly visible to the south as you skirt the edge of Tyndall Glacier. Use caution here and do not approach the glacier's edge. The scramble up the side of Hallett is short but steep.

The top of Hallett is strewn with boulders. To the south is a five-foot-high cairn, and on the northern edge, just east of a wall of stacked boulders, is the geologic survey marker, proudly proclaiming that you are at 12,713 feet. If weather permits, enjoy a much-deserved lunch as you drink in the panoramic views.

Return via the same route; take your time and exercise caution when descending the rock field.

TRAILHEAD

Ranger Station

Bear Lake

Nymph Lake

Glacier Gorge Junction

Dream Lake

Glacier Creek

Lake Haiyaha

Emerald Lake

Gorge

Dream Gorge

Tyndall

Flattop Mountain

Tyndall Glacier

Hallett Peak

Lake Helene

N

P · A · R · K

9800

9800

10400

10800

10400

11000

11200

11200

11200

11800

12200

12400

12100

FLATTOP MOUNTAIN AND HALLETT PEAK   45

9. Greyrock Trail

BY ED SEELY

MAPS	Trails Illustrated, Cache La Poudre/ Big Thompson, Number 101 USGS, Poudre Park 7.5 minute
ELEVATION GAIN	2,056 feet
RATING	Moderate
ROUND-TRIP DISTANCE	6 miles
ROUND-TRIP TIME	6 hours at moderate pace
NEAREST LANDMARK	Ted's Place, at the junction of U.S. 287 and Colorado 14

COMMENT: This is a heavily used and very popular trail that is easily accessible from Fort Collins. The summit of Greyrock is of geologic interest: It is a massive granitic intrusion that has weathered to its rounded shape through exfoliation. The summit block provides popular rock-climbing routes. Watch for poison ivy along the way. The trail near the summit is not marked, and over the years hikers have become lost and required rescue help. Dogs on leash are permitted.

GETTING THERE: Take U.S. 287 north from Fort Collins about 10 miles to the Colorado 14 junction at Ted's Place. Go west on Colorado 14 about 8.6 miles to the Greyrock parking area located on the left (south) side of the highway.

THE ROUTE: From the parking lot, take the stairs down to the highway; cross carefully, as traffic can be fast moving. Take the scenic footbridge over the Poudre River to the trailhead. The trail maintains an easy grade to the lower junction with the Meadows Trail. Turn right at the lower junction to ascend the main trail along the creek. As the trail climbs the drainage, note the protective rock walls that were built during the Civilian Conservation Corps (CCC) days following the Great Depression. Respect this historic work by not walking on the walls. As you near the upper junction, a rock outcrop on the left

Greyrock summit from Upper Junction.

provides a place to catch your breath and a nice overlook back down the valley. From the overlook, it is about twenty minutes farther, at a moderate pace, to the upper junction. Greyrock Peak first comes into view a short distance past this overlook. There will be a bit of elevation loss next, followed by several switchbacks leading to an open meadow and the upper junction with the Meadows Trail. This upper junction is a great spot to appreciate the bulk of Greyrock Peak. You may begin to hear voices of rock climbers at this point. After a short level stretch, the trail begins to climb along the eastern side of the peak. In places, the trail is not obvious, but rock cairns may be visible to help you stay on track. The U.S. Forest Service (USFS) has also installed several reassurance posts to help you locate the trail.

Southwestern view of the far Rockies from Greyrock summit.

Near elevation contour 7400, the trail turns back to the south-west and tops out in the summit area. You will want to note this point for your return. If the weather has not been exceptionally dry, you will see some small lakes here.

There is no marked trail from here to the peak but, again, cairns may be visible. Cross to the southwest to begin to climb to the peak. Some scrambling and walking on sloping rock slabs is required to reach the peak, but you will be rewarded with exciting views. The plains are clearly visible to the east, with the numerous lakes of Fort Collins glinting in the sunlight earlier in the day. Snowcapped mountains are visible to the south in the Mummy Range and in the Rawahs to the west. If you start early, this is a great place to have lunch; if the weather looks threatening, have only a quick snack and begin your descent.

On your descent, take care to retrace your upward route; the descent offers the greatest likelihood of getting off trail. Continue to watch for the small rock cairns and reassurance posts.

10. Hewlett Gulch

BY SANDY JORDAN

MAPS	Trails Illustrated, Cache La Poudre/ Big Thompson, Number 101
ELEVATION GAIN	1,070 feet
RATING	Easy–moderate
ROUND-TRIP DISTANCE	7.8 miles
ROUND-TRIP TIME	3–4 hours
NEAREST LANDMARK	Ted's Place, at the junction of U.S. 287 and Colorado 14

COMMENT: The longest part of the popular Hewlett Gulch Trail is an easy hike, with about twenty shallow crossings through Gordon Creek. The trail follows the gulch for about 2 miles and then forms a 3.7-mile loop. In the first mile of trail, there are several stone foundations dating back to the early 1900s. Poppies and lilac bushes in this area are likely the remains of horticultural efforts by the early settlers.

Hewlett Gulch Trail offers one of the most enjoyable hikes in the lower Poudre Canyon. The profusion of wildflowers and butterflies in the spring can put a hiker on visual overload. Although the usual cautions exist for mountain lions, snakes, and bears, hikers are more likely to see fox, deer, songbirds, and lots of squirrels. The first couple of miles are easy enough for families with youngsters to enjoy. Dogs under voice control are allowed.

The trail is well populated on weekends by both two- and four-legged hikers and is also a favorite of mountain bikers. (One biker described the trail to me as "moderately technical and awesome"). Users of all kinds and species seem to respect one another, and I have never had a negative encounter on the trail.

Winter sports enthusiasts, including hard-core bikers, also find Hewlett Gulch Trail delightful. Gordon Creek adds to winter's ambience with ice-glazed rocks and frozen ripples layering over the running brook.

Hewlett Gulch trailhead.

PHOTO BY SANDY JORDAN

GETTING THERE: Take U.S. 287 north from Fort Collins about 10 miles to the Colorado 14 junction at Ted's Place. Go west on Colorado 14 about 10 miles, or 0.6 mile beyond mile marker 112. This is about 1.5 miles beyond the Greyrock Trail parking area, not far beyond the community of Poudre Park. To your right, a short bridge crosses the river and a dirt road on the left goes to the parking area and trailhead. There is a well-maintained restroom at the trailhead.

THE ROUTE: About forty-five minutes from the start of the hike, a junction with a false trail rises sharply to the left. This should not be confused with the actual loop trail, and a fallen tree trunk or branches usually discourage hikers from this option.

A short distance ahead, the trail drops about 10 feet and quickly rises again. The actual junction for the loop is just beyond this depression and is clearly marked with a rock cairn. Hikers seeking a very rigorous, steep, and rocky climb can take this left turn to begin the loop. Those of fainter heart

Water break at Gordon Creek.   PHOTO BY SANDY JORDAN

and mellower disposition should continue along the trail; you can choose that segment of the loop on the return (downhill) portion of the trip.

Once you are past the loop junction, you will experience a rather moderate climb. About an hour into your hike, the trail narrows into a steep and rocky but short climb, then opens into a vast meadow. Here the trail becomes a double track on a moderately inclined path, merging alternately to single track up to the summit.

The trail eventually appears to end at a "T," but observant hikers will notice a left turn to complete the loop. Taking the trail to the right will lead to an overlook near Diamond Rock. You can look down upon the Poudre River and Colorado 14 from this overlook, but there is no access to the parking area or the highway from here. Thus, take the left turn to stay on the loop and to begin your return portion of the hike.

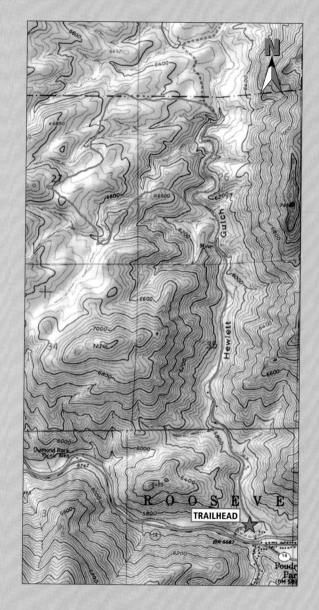

TRAILHEAD

R O O S E V E

11. Horsetooth Rock

BY JOHN GASCOYNE

MAPS	Larimer County Parks and Open Lands
ELEVATION GAIN	1,500 feet
RATING	Moderate
ROUND-TRIP DISTANCE	5 miles
ROUND-TRIP TIME	3–4 hours
NEAREST LANDMARK	Horsetooth Reservoir

COMMENT: We asked ten Fort Collins residents to name the area's best-known landmark, and nine of them replied that it has to be Horsetooth Rock. (The tenth person arrived only three days ago and, strictly speaking, should not have been included in our survey.) Horsetooth Rock is not only visible and impressive from miles away, it also provides a close-in and very enjoyable hike. Normally mild winters in the foothills mean that you can hike the area throughout much of the year.

The Horsetooth Rock Trail is part of a system of trails located in Horsetooth Mountain Park, a nearly 3,000-acre area rolling across the foothills above Horsetooth Reservoir. You can spend many enjoyable days at the park exploring the various other trail options, including one that takes you out of the Horsetooth Mountain Park north to Lory State Park.

Horsetooth Mountain Park is open to hikers, bikers, horseback riders, and dogs on leashes. Most folks observe the right-of-way rules: horses having the right-of-way over hikers and bikers, hikers having the right-of-way over bikers.

This is a fee area—six dollars per passenger vehicle. Restrooms and drinking water are available in the parking area. This is a popular area, especially on weekends, so it is probably best to arrive early.

As with most foothill areas, there is some potential here for encounters with wildlife, including the creatures that we are trained to fear: bears, mountain lions, and rattlesnakes. It is prudent to exercise normal caution and to maintain

Horsetooth Rock, Fort Collins best-known landmark.   PHOTO BY JOHN GASCOYNE

supervision over young people. It is also mandatory to rejoice in having so much of nature, even the exciting parts, so readily available to us.

GETTING THERE: From Fort Collins, take Taft Hill Road to Harmony Road and turn west onto County Road 38E. Stay on 38E for about 6.5 miles, going around the south end of Horsetooth Reservoir and continuing west to Horsetooth Mountain Park parking area, on your right.

THE ROUTE: At the trailhead, you will have a choice of either the Soderberg Trail or the somewhat shorter service road, both of which will lead you to the Horsetooth Rock Trail. There are some side-trail possibilities, but it is recommended that you stay on the main trail for your first ascent. Markers indicate the summit approach, so there is little likelihood of going off trail. When you arrive at the memorial marker of a young climber, you will be looking at three trail options. Take the middle, broader path. The approach to the base of Horsetooth Rock itself requires a bit of easy scrambling. When you have another option, stay to your right (the northwesterly direc-

Looking south and east from the norther summit.   PHOTO BY JOHN GASCOYNE

tion). This approach is easier than the southern, or left-handed, choice. Some bouldering, with a bit of exposure, will be necessary to reach the top of the rock. The left-handed trail will lead to the more southern "tooth" and a somewhat more challenging bouldering situation. On the return trip, you can explore the Audra Culver Trail as an alternative way down.

Horsetooth
Mountain

MOUNTAIN PARK

Spring

6800

6400

6528

6864

6200

6510

6000

6400

6600

36

6000

6000

6132

5762

BM

TRAILHEAD

5800

5800

5652

6000

N

1

12. Montgomery Pass Trail (#986)

BY JOE AND FRÉDÉRIQUE GRIM

MAPS	Trails Illustrated, Poudre River/ Cameron Pass, Number 112 USGS, Clark Peak 7.5 minute
ELEVATION GAIN	1,049 feet
RATING	Moderate but short
ROUND-TRIP DISTANCE	3.8 miles
ROUND-TRIP TIME	3 hours
NEAREST LANDMARK	Cameron Pass

COMMENT: This is a four-season trail that quickly takes you above timberline as it climbs up to Montgomery Pass. The trail provides an enjoyable short hike in the summer, and it can serve as a good jumping-off point for longer trips to nearby peaks in the Medicine Bow Range, such as Diamond Peaks and Clark Peak. In the winter, the trail is popular with snowshoers and backcountry skiers on their way up to the bowls of Diamond Peaks. The climb up to the pass is pleasant as you pass through evergreen forest interspersed with a few small meadows. The pass itself is the prize, however, as it has magnificent views of the surrounding peaks and ranges and down into North Park. But don't just focus your sights on the mountain vistas; a host of beautiful alpine flowers grow here in the late spring and into early summer.

GETTING THERE: From Fort Collins, go north about 10 miles on U.S. 287 to Ted's Place and turn left (west) onto Colorado 14. Follow Colorado 14 up the Cache la Poudre Canyon 56.4 miles to the Zimmerman Lake trailhead. The trail begins on the opposite side of the road, on the north side of the parking lot, and is indicated by a small sign.

THE ROUTE: The trail begins at an elevation of 9,987 feet. Start by gradually climbing to the north, generally paralleling the highway, while making your way through spruce forest. At

Montgomery Pass in winter.

PHOTO BY JOE GRIM

Montgomery Creek, turn sharply left and head upstream, following an old jeep road along the creek. Here the trail starts to climb moderately toward the west. After half a mile, you leave the creek and climb more steeply for a while, along a ridge. As the trail gets higher, you will pass through a few small meadows. At the 1.4 mile mark, you will reach the remnants of an old cabin that some believe belonged to settler Tom Montgomery around 1900. Just past the cabin is a sign that says to turn right to go to Montgomery Pass. (Turning left and following the signage "to the bowls" would take you steeply up to timberline and to an old mine. This is the route frequently taken by backcountry skiers to reach "the bowls," which lie further to the south, below Diamond Peaks. Be aware: There can be significant avalanche danger in the bowls, and fatalities have occurred there in the past. It is critical to check avalanche conditions before you leave.) From here, the climb becomes less steep and, after .33-mile, you will reach timberline and, shortly after, Montgomery Pass and an elevation of 10,998 feet. The views from the pass are awesome. You can see down

Flowers, trees, and mountains—why we love to hike.

PHOTO BY JOE GRIM

into North Park and across to the Park Range. Looking in the other direction, you can view the Mummy Range to the southeast and the Never Summer Range to the south.

You can turn around here or continue to hike from the pass. To the south of the pass is a faint trail that leads to the old mine and to the trail that goes to the end of the bowls. You can also reach the 11,700-foot Diamond Peaks by following the ridgeline south for 1.5 miles. A faint jeep trail along the ridge leads to the identically named Montgomery Pass Trail, in Colorado State Forest State Park. Continue to follow the ridgeline five miles to the north to arrive at Clark Peak; at 12,951 feet, this is the sentinel of the Medicine Bow Range.

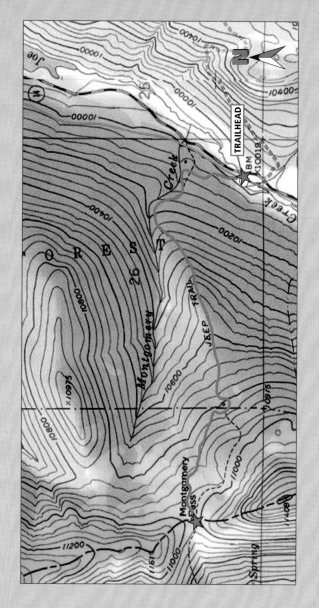

13. Mount Margaret

BY JOHN GASCOYNE

MAPS	Trails Illustrated, Red Feather Lakes/ Glendevy. Number 111
ELEVATION GAIN	Minus 137 feet
RATING	Easy
ROUND-TRIP DISTANCE	8 miles
ROUND-TRIP TIME	3–4 hours
NEAREST LANDMARK	Red Feather

COMMENT: "This is what I call solvency," my friend exclaimed as he finished a 360-degree pirouette on the top of Mount Margaret. This was the lead-in to a lunch-break discussion of how we can never go broke as long as the striking views, the chipmunks skittering across the rocks, an eagle windsurfing a thermal updraft, and restorative solitude remain available to us at such places. Forget that the crest of Mount Margaret is lower than the trailhead and that there is little perceptible elevation change between the two. When you reach the top, it feels like the top. Oh yes, ascending to the very, very top is not at all recommended: It consists of a dome about 30 feet high and, without climbing gear, could not be scaled without significant exposure.

GETTING THERE: From the intersection of Shields and U.S. 287 on the northwest side of Fort Collins, go 17 miles west and then north on U.S. 287 (going past the turnoff to Poudre Canyon) to the Livermore Junction. Turn left on to County Road 74E; go 20 more miles and watch for the trailhead parking lot on your right. Note that you will be asked to close the gate behind you; cattle graze this part of the Roosevelt National Forest.

THE ROUTE: The trail to Mount Margaret is straightforward and there is generally good signage where other trails intersect with the main trail. Early on in your hike, you will come to a medium-size stream. To avoid wading, look for a narrow path

Mount Margaret Trail, close to the summit.   PHOTO BY JOHN GASCOYNE

somewhat to your right once you have the stream in sight. This will take you to a narrow but stable footbridge over the stream. Bear to your left after crossing and you will be back on the trail. Another mile or so will bring you to another gate and another chance to practice bovine etiquette on the trail. Shortly after, there is a fork in the path, and you will want to stay to the right. About 2.5 miles along the trail, you will come to what some maps describe as the Five Points intersection. You have an array of trail choices here, two on your left that lead to Dowdy Lake and one that is part of a loop trail off of

An unlikely rock formation.   PHOTO BY JOHN GASCOYNE

the main trail. A soft right turn will keep you on the main
trail; a nearby sign will verify that you are on the proper path.
For the most part, the trail to Mount Margaret feels very open
and more like you are hiking the high plains rather than a
mountainous path. As you begin to move up to the summit,
however, you will experience a somewhat abrupt change in the
topography and feel more like you are in the high Colorado
mountains. As you sit at the summit contemplating the wonderful view, consider that you are more than 100 feet lower
than the trailhead where you started. This seeming incon-
gruity only tells us that there is a gradual and barely recogniz-
able downslope throughout much of the trail.

Shorter routes to Mount Margaret are possible by driving
past the trailhead, then going through Red Feather and on to
Dowdy Lake. Depending upon which of two alternative trails
you take, you can shave at least a mile from the 4-mile hike
to the top.

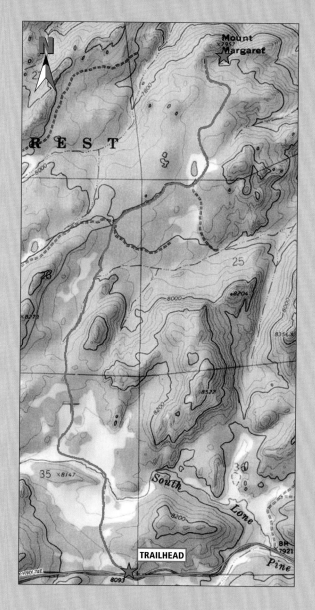

Mount
Margaret

R E S T

TRAILHEAD

14. Mount McConnell

BY LISA BARKLEY
PHOTOS BY ANDREW C. GORIS

MAPS	Trails Illustrated, Cache La Poudre/ Big Thompson, Number 100 (2003 version has errors) USGS, Big Narrows, Roosevelt National Forest 7.5 minute
ELEVATION GAIN	1,327 feet
RATING	Easy to moderate
ROUND-TRIP DISTANCE	4.8 miles
ROUND-TRIP TIME	4 hours
NEAREST LANDMARK	Ted's Place, at the junction of U.S. 287 and Colorado 14

COMMENT: The McConnell Summit Trail is a short and scenic loop hike in the Cache La Poudre Wilderness, with great views of the Poudre Canyon, Poudre River, and surrounding mountain ranges.

There is a four-dollar fee for day use; drinking water and restrooms are available at the trailhead. Although the parking lot is closed in winter, the lower elevation of the area makes hiking possible during most of the year. Caution should be used in winter months, however, as much of the trail is north facing and may have snow. Dogs on a leash are allowed.

The Cache La Poudre Wilderness is a small wilderness area of 9,400 acres and is crossed by the Poudre River and the Little South Fork of the Poudre River. Mount McConnell and Bear Mountain are the only two named peaks in the wilderness area, according to the USGS map. There are only two maintained trails in the area: the McConnell Summit Trail, described here, and the Kreutzer Nature Trail. The Summit Trail loops off of the Kreutzer Trail.

GETTING THERE: From downtown Fort Collins, head north about 10 miles on U.S. 287 until you reach Ted's Place, at the junction

The view from Mount McConnell.

PHOTO BY ANDREW C. GORIS

with Colorado 14. Turn left and go west on Colorado 14 for about 23.5 miles. Turn left off of Colorado 14 and cross a bridge over the Poudre River to the Mountain Park Recreation Area sign. Make an immediate right turn to the parking lot.

THE ROUTE: Start from the trailhead at the lower parking lot and hike the loop in a counterclockwise direction. The trail ascends steeply with numerous switchbacks. Just short of the 0.5 mile point, there is an overlook of the campground. As you ascend the trail, you will view the Poudre River, the surrounding mountains, and Colorado 14 to the north. The switchbacks will continue.

At 0.8 mile, you will reach a junction for the Kreutzer Nature Trail. Turn right (west) to stay on the McConnell Trail (marked as Trail #992). For the quicker loop, keep going straight on the Kreutzer Trail (Trail #936). At a bit over a mile, you'll see a scree field. At the edge of this field is a small rock

The columbine, our State flower.

wall that can be used as a rest area or as a good site to take photos of your hiking companions.

At 1.25 miles, the trail opens up and provides wonderful views, including the Mummy Range to the west. A 300-foot side trail branches off to the west and rewards you with a bird's-eye view of the Poudre River down below.

You'll find interesting rock formations as you continue on. At nearly 2 miles, the trail branches right (west) to the McConnell summit. At slightly more than 2 miles, you reach the summit and can enjoy a panoramic overlook. This is a great place to relax; large boulders provide several places to get out of the wind, if that is a factor.

From here, backtrack to the main trail to continue. (Distances beyond this point include the round trip to the summit.) After a short way, you'll find an interesting rock bench on the left and a short spur going to another nice view.

The trip down is steeper and more rugged than the ascent. This section makes the hike a bit more challenging, but it is worth the effort. However, if you want to avoid this portion, you could make this an out-and-back hike by going to the summit and returning on the same section of trail.

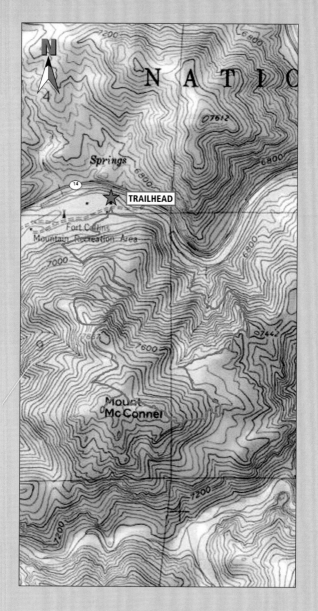

15. Pawnee Buttes

BY EILEEN EDELMAN
PHOTOS BY SUSAN FRIEDMAN

MAPS	USGS, Pawnee Buttes, Grover SW 7.5 minute
ELEVATION GAIN	Minus 200 feet
RATING	Easy
ROUND-TRIP DISTANCE	4 miles
ROUND-TRIP TIME	4 hours (longer during wildflower season)
NEAREST LANDMARK	I-25 and Colorado 14

COMMENT: The Pawnee Buttes are two enormous, capped sandstone structures, remnants of an ancient sea that once covered this now arid area. Mini-badlands, smaller rock towers, and fascinating plains ecology surround them. When you hike there, you will see exciting wildflowers and birds as you wander through terrain so strange that parts of it can feel as if you are walking on the surface of the moon.

GETTING THERE: The drive from the east side of Fort Collins takes about ninety minutes. From downtown, go east on Colorado 14 (Mulberry Street) over Interstate 25 (exit 269A), and proceed east for 37 miles to the turnoff for Briggsdale. Turn left (north) on County Road 77 and drive 15 miles, then turn right (east) on County Road 120 and go 6 miles to Grover. Go through Grover and then turn right (east) on County Road 390 for 6 miles. Turn left on County Road 112 for 6 more miles. At the "T," turn right and continue following signs for the next 3 miles to the trailhead.

THE ROUTE: The trail begins by heading east and down an open meadow, bursting with flowers during the spring and early summer. In about ten minutes, you will come to a gap in a fence; shortly afterwards, there is a fork in the trail. The path to the right climbs to the top of a ridge and is closed in the

Pawnee Buttes, where the resistant Ogallala Formation caps the top of the buttes, protecting the softer White River formation. PHOTO BY SUSAN FRIEDMAN

springtime to protect nesting raptors. Take the left trail, which soon descends into the area of mini-badlands. You will drop below the level of the grasses and go back up again several times. Strange rock formations surround you, and you will pass one large tower resembling a shark's fin constructed out of mud. Toward the end of this section is a clump of juniper, possibly the only shady area on the hike. A number of gullies will cross your path in this area, so be careful not to make an unplanned detour.

About thirty minutes from the trailhead, you will come back to the surface level permanently and will be walking on a wide gravel road. The West Butte is on your left, and you will soon pass the other end of the trail over the ridge. Your trail then curves around the east side of the butte to a large bare area with views east to the plains; continue toward the East Butte. You will pass a sign advising you that the trail passes through private lands. It is about a ten-minute walk from the bare area to the base of the East Butte. If the day is very windy,

On the Buttes Trail.

you will be glad to discover a series of gullies on the right, where you can descend and get out of the wind for lunch.

Right at the base of the butte is a good path that goes off to the left and begins to circle the butte in a clockwise direction. Follow this, and in about five minutes, the path will climb partway up the butte. The first ledges you reach provide photo-ops and a lovely perch for lunch. If you are surefooted and not worried about sun exposure, you can continue on the path. The views you will come to are incredible: You will be looking out over the plains, down into more moonscape-style badlands, and, finally, back across at the West Butte. After you have circumnavigated the butte, descend with caution, as the surface of the rock is coated with dried, rather crumbly mud. You will now find yourself back at the foot of the East Butte. The West Butte is in front of you. Retrace your steps and you should be back at your car within an hour.

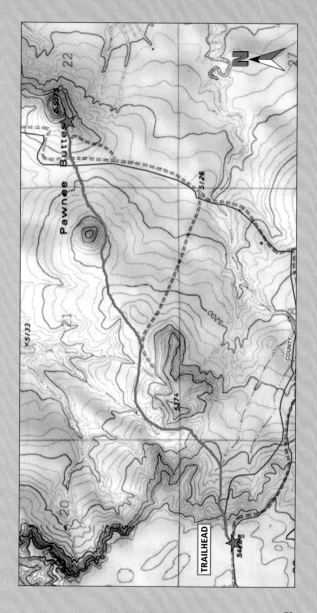

TRAILHEAD

Pawnee Buttes

22

26

21

33

20

16. Poudre Trail

BY YORK, THE RED LION

MAPS	Fort Collins city maps; local bicycling maps
ELEVATION GAIN	182 feet
RATING	Easy
ROUND-TRIP DISTANCE	22 miles
ROUND-TRIP TIME	2–3 hours by bicycle
NEAREST LANDMARK	Downtown Fort Collins

COMMENT: The Poudre Trail is an 11-mile pathway through much of the best that Fort Collins has to offer. It provides access to outdoor art, local history, natural areas, and, of course, the Poudre River. The many transportation options include wheelchairs, road bikes and mountain bikes, running and walking shoes, roller blades, skateboards, and horses. You can explore this riverside corridor in three sections, from southeast to downtown to northwest of the city.

Our adventure will begin at the southeast terminus, Colorado State University's Environmental Learning Center (ELC). After a few miles of this wild and winding beginning, you'll work your way along the north side of Fort Collins to Martinez Park. From this midpoint, the trail goes mostly to the west and somewhat to the north to end at Lyons Park, close to LaPorte.

GETTING THERE: You can access the Poudre Trail at Lyons Park, Martinez Park, or at numerous other locations along the way. To get to our starting point—the ELP trailhead—from downtown Fort Collins, go south on College Avenue, or any other major north-south roadway, to Drake Road. Go left on Drake and proceed east until the road ends, just past the water filtration plant on your left. At the canal, turn left on to the dirt road and go about 0.25 mile to the ELC parking lot. There is ample parking and an outdoor restroom at this trailhead.

The Poudre Trail at Lions Park.   PHOTO BY JOHN GASCOYNE

THE ROUTE: Not far from the trailhead, a canal crossing marks the East Drake Pondworks, a thought-provoking component of the city's Art in Public Places (APP) program. As you follow the winding trail, you'll pass by reclaimed gravel pit fishing ponds and, a bit farther, shady resting spots and small side trails leading to the river. There is abundant wildlife in this area and you can look for beavers, fox, rabbits, squirrels, deer, raccoons, turtles, ospreys, and other larger birds.

At 1.5 miles from the ELC, there is a junction with the Spring Creek Trail. Here also are an emergency call box and maps of the city's trail system. Go northwest from the junction, stopping along the way to appreciate the APP installation, Ripple Effects, before crossing under Timberline and on to the Kingfisher Point Natural Area.

Continue west under the Lemay Bridge and go up the ramp on your left. Once you are on Lemay, proceed north across the bridge and pick up the trail just as you are approaching the highway intersection. When you reach Linden Street, south of

New Belgium Brewery, go across the street and to the south end of the bridge to pick up the trail.

Another mile or so will take you to Martinez Park, the midpoint of the trail. As you continue west, you'll begin to see the history of past water projects: canals, cisterns, diversion dams, bridges, spillways, and water drops—all reminders of the important role of water in this area's history.

Close to the eastern terminus.

The western section of the trail begins when you cross under Shields Street. The next mile is punctuated by informational signage about the Cache La Poudre River National Area and by views ranging from Longs Peak to Grey Rock Mountain. The Taft Hill Road parking area provides a solar air pump, a picnic table, and an emergency call box. Exercise caution when crossing this busy road. The next 0.75-mile stretch, with power poles, a sometimes-noisy gravel conveyor, and no tree cover, has to be the least enchanting portion of the entire trail. Abruptly, you will encounter the river again at the Butterfly Woods Natural Area. The long, multidirectional bridge that takes you over the river is an architectural treat and, at the same time, yields excellent views up and downstream.

After crossing under the Overland Trail Bridge, you enter Lyons Park and the end of the City of Fort Collins trail. Restrooms, picnic tables with barbecue stoves, an air pump, and parking are all available at this park, which closes at sunset. West of the park, the trail continues on to LaPorte and provides access to many more biking and hiking trails.

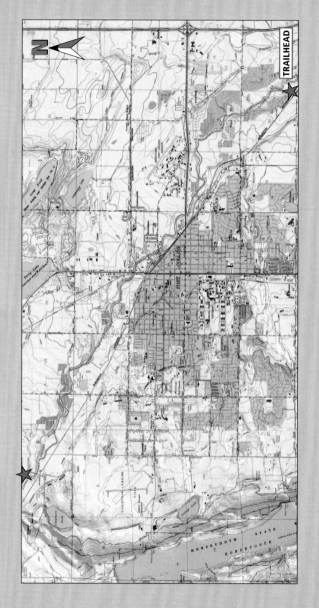

17. Stormy Peaks Trail to Stormy Peaks Pass

BY JEFF EISELE

MAPS	Trails Illustrated, Poudre River/ Cameron Pass, Number 112 USGS, Pingree Park 7.5 minute
ELEVATION GAIN	2,700 feet
RATING	Moderate
ROUND-TRIP DISTANCE	11.2 miles
ROUND-TRIP TIME	6–8 hours
NEAREST LANDMARK	Ted's Place at the junction of U.S. 287 and Colorado 14

COMMENT: The Stormy Peaks Trail to Stormy Peaks Pass begins in Roosevelt National Forest near the entrance to Colorado State University's Pingree Park mountain campus. It travels through portions of the national forest, the Comanche Peak Wilderness, and north Rocky Mountain National Park.

Hikers who wish to continue beyond this described hike, to the Stormy Peaks summits, will scramble over grassy slopes and large boulders an additional 0.2 mile and 475 feet higher to the west summit at 12,148 feet. After that, it's another 0.5 mile with an additional 50 feet of climbing to the east summit at 11,986 feet.

This well-defined trail offers a wide variety of hiking experiences, traveling through part of the 1994 Hourglass Fire burn area, where new growth is established. It then goes through aspen, spruce, and lodgepole pine forest on to timberline and rolling tundra abundant with wildflowers.

Your hike includes expansive views of the Mummy Range and the Never Summer Range to the west and north. The drainage of the North Fork of the Poudre River is visible to the north and, in its upper reaches, panoramas of the Front Range foothills. To the south, you will have vistas of Rocky Mountain National Park (RMNP).

Picture perfect on the Stormy Peak Trail. PHOTO BY JEFF EISELE

GETTING THERE: From downtown Fort Collins, go north on U.S. 287 about 10 miles to Ted's Place, then turn left and go west on Colorado 14 for approximately 26 miles to County Road 63E, also known as the Pingree Park Road. Turn left and go south on County Road 63E approximately 16 miles to the Stormy Peak trailhead. (Note that after 12 miles, County Road 63E merges with County Road 44H.) The trailhead parking lot is across the road from the Pingree Park campus entrance. In good conditions, your drive will take about 90 minutes.

THE ROUTE: After four switchbacks in the first 0.5 mile, the rocky trail follows a mostly south-southwest path for 2.7 miles, then goes in a south-southeasterly direction to the pass. It crosses junctions with trails to Denny's Point, at 0.6 mile from the trailhead, and Twin Lakes Reservoir, at 0.9 mile. At 2.7 miles from the beginning, you will enter the wilderness and then, after 3.5 miles, RMNP. Dogs are not allowed on the trail after this point.

Approximately 4.3 miles into the hike, rock cairns begin to mark the route and help guide you through the only area where you might stray off trail.

Why we love Colorado.   PHOTO BY JEFF EISELE

The Stormy Peaks North campsite is at 4.5 miles and just beyond, at 4.7 miles, timberline begins at an elevation of 11,000 feet. A backcountry/wilderness permit from RMNP is required for overnight stays at the campsite.

From here to the pass, you will hike through tundra with a wide variety of wildflowers in spring and summer. Columbine, bluebells, Indian paintbrush, cinquefoil, and many other flowers color the landscape.

As you continue, look to the east for a summit with a large boulder seemingly balanced on end. This is a false summit. The true west Stormy Peaks summit is farther east and comes into view as you near the pass.

At the pass, with the summits beyond, you can peer into the valley where the North Fork of the Big Thompson River runs. You can also see Comanche Peak and Fall Mountain to the northwest and, to the south and southwest, Mount Dickinson, Mount Dunraven, Mummy Mountain, Hagues Peak, Rowe Peak, and Rowe Mountain.

From the pass, follow the same route back to the trailhead.

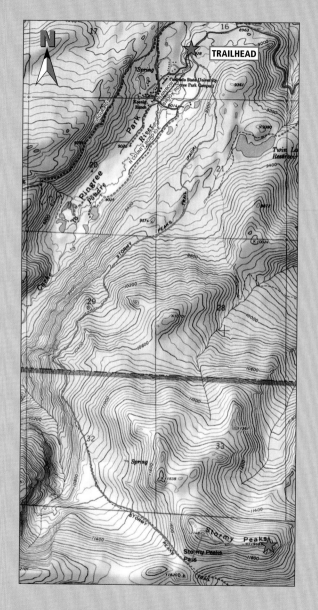

18. Trap Park

BY PAUL WEBER

MAPS	Trails Illustrated, Poudre River/Cameron Pass, Number 112 USGS, Chambers Lake 7.5 minute
ELEVATION GAIN	600 feet
RATING	Moderate
ROUND-TRIP DISTANCE	6.2 miles
ROUND-TRIP TIME	4 hours
NEAREST LANDMARK	Cameron Pass

COMMENT: From cool fir forest to a sun-filled valley with abundant water and wildflowers, surrounded by the Neota Wilderness, this hike has it all. This quiet valley offers opportunities for backcountry camping in an open meadow, with views of Iron and Flattop mountains and Trap Creek whispering in the background. Moose and other wildlife frequently can be seen.

The trail travels up the valley to the boundary of the Neota Wilderness Area, which encompasses the upper valley and ridges along both sides but excludes the valley floor. The views are impressive after the first mile, so shorter hikes are still worthwhile. The Long Draw Road is closed in winter, so enjoy this hike between June and October.

GETTING THERE: From downtown Fort Collins, drive about 10 miles north on U.S. 287 to Ted's Place and turn left (west) on Colorado 14. Travel 53 miles up Poudre Canyon to Long Draw Road (Forest Service Road 156) on your left. Go 3 miles to the Trap Creek trailhead parking on the right. There are no restroom facilities at the trailhead, but a vault toilet is located at a parking area on the left side of Colorado 14, 0.1 mile before Long Draw Road.

THE ROUTE: This trail follows a long, closed road that once provided access to Trap Park. Just a few minutes from the parking lot trailhead, the trail turns left into a short switchback

A lush marsh surrounds a small pond along the Trap Park Trail.

through a boulder field and a view of Trap Lake and Clark Peak in the Rawah Wilderness Area. You then enter a canyon, with Trap Creek rushing below. Next, the trail crosses a small, unnamed stream in a quiet forest of Douglas fir and spruce. After 1 mile, the trail emerges from the canyon with a view up the valley toward Iron Mountain.

To the left, a short path leads up a knoll to camping sites, while on the right, the trail crosses Trap Creek to continue

Iron Mountain, 12,265 feet, as visible from the trail. PHOTO BY PAUL WEBER

southwest up the valley. Across the creek, the trail slopes
gradually upward for another 2 miles along the right side of
the valley floor. The open meadow provides views of Flattop
Mountain on the southeastern ridgeline, while Iron Mountain
presides over the upper valley. The trail crosses the creek twice
near the upper terminus. Then, at a small cluster of tall fir,
signage announcing the boundary of the Neota Wilderness
Area marks the end of the trail. Return to the trailhead via the
same route.

N

NATIONAL

Bald
Mountain

TRAILHEAD ★

Park   Creek

Trap

Trap

Flat Top
Mountain

★

19. Twin Crater Lakes

BY DAVID WASSON

MAPS	Trails Illustrated, Poudre Canyon/ Cameron Pass, Number 112 USFS, Rawah Lakes, Boston Peak
ELEVATION GAIN	2,500 feet
RATING	Moderate
ROUND-TRIP DISTANCE	13 miles
ROUND-TRIP TIME	6–8 hours
NEAREST LANDMARK	Cameron Pass

COMMENT: Twin Crater Lakes are near the middle of the Rawah Wilderness Area and provide a full-day hike through old-growth forests to a rewarding destination below steep, rocky ridges and mountain summits. Sturdy log bridges allow crossings of the West Branch of the Laramie River. In early summer, flower lovers can enjoy an array of beautiful displays from wild iris and penstemon to avalanche lilies and Jacob's ladder. Birding enthusiasts may spot a red-naped sapsucker, pygmy nuthatch, or broad-tailed hummingbird. Big-game sightings include deer, elk, moose, and bighorn sheep. In the higher elevations of the Rawahs, snow can remain into early summer, and access to the trailhead via the Laramie River Road is limited by snow closure for several months each year.

If you want to extend your hike beyond the Twin Crater Lakes, following the West Branch Trail to its terminus will lead to Carey Lake and Island Lake. These lakes offer another beautiful destination for a full-day trip in the Rawahs, with outstanding views of Cameron Peak, at 12,127 feet, and Clark Peak, at 12,951 feet.

Hot summer days can bring mosquitoes from the still water in the area, so plan ahead and pack insect repellent. These trails are horse-friendly and you may encounter equestrians while you are hiking. Fires are prohibited above timberline in the Rawah Wilderness.

A 12,240' ridge rises above Twin Crater Lakes and the
North Fork Trail.

PHOTO BY DAVID WASSON

GETTING THERE: From Fort Collins, head north on U.S. 287 for
about 10 miles to Ted's Place. Turn left (west) on Colorado 14
and go 52 miles to the Laramie River Road. Turn right (north)
and follow the road 7 miles, passing Tunnel Campground, to
the West Branch trailhead. Toilets are available at the trailhead.

THE ROUTE: From the trailhead, the West Branch Trail heads
south alongside the road and turns west for a short distance,
then crosses a large bridge south to the dirt trail. Your hike
continues west as a pleasant route in the Rawah Wilderness
Area. As the trail continues west, it crosses several small
streams in the first 2.5 miles before reaching the Camp Lake
Trail. Continue southwest on the West Branch Trail along a
gentler grade for another mile, where the trail will intersect
with the Rawah Trail. Take the Rawah Trail west and enjoy the
old-growth spruce and fir forests in this wild area.

Aspen along the west branch of the Laramie River.

After a mile, the trail rises more steeply and crosses two wide log bridges. Continue up the switchbacks to the intersection with the North Fork Trail. Turn left, heading southwest on this trail until you reach timberline and a splendid view of steep ridges in the Rawahs. The high falls on the ridge to the northwest drain from Rockhole Lake, at 11,200 feet. South Rawah Peak rises above, at 12,644 feet. Continue on the trail, heading southwest, and stay on the west side of the drainage. The trail turns, and you will go south until you near the first of Twin Crater Lakes. The diamond-shaped high point on the ridge, at 11,680 feet, provides a dramatic backdrop to your adventure. To return, retrace your route back to the trailhead.

Laramie

N

20. Vedauwoo/Turtle Rock Loop

BY ANN HUNT

MAPS	USGS, Sherman Mountains east 7.5 minute USGS, Sherman Mountains west 7.5 minute
ELEVATION GAIN	Less than 100 feet
RATING	Easy
ROUND-TRIP DISTANCE	2.8 miles
ROUND-TRIP TIME	1.5 hours
NEAREST LANDMARK	Laramie, Wyoming

COMMENT: The Vedauwoo (VAY-duh-voo) area, "land of the earth-born spirit" in the Arapaho dialect, is a wonderful array of stunning granite formations that both intrigue the eye and beckon the body to try a bit of rock scrambling. This 7,600-acre oasis sits on the Wyoming high plains at an elevation of 8,000 feet. Ponderosa pine, Douglas fir, and aspen trees add to Vedauwoo's natural beauty. The aspen trees offer a golden delight in the early autumn. The area is home to small mammals, deer, antelope, and domestic cattle. The winds seem to always blow, sculpting the land and giving soaring rides to the native raptors that nest in many hideaways among the rock pinnacles. This is a good destination for all seasons: spring, summer, and fall hiking, rock climbing, and camping—both in established and at primitive sites. In winter, you can enjoy crosscountry skiing and snowshoeing.

The dramatic landscape invites the casual and professional photographer in every season, and extraordinary views of granite spires and domes provide unique photo opportunities. Vedauwoo is a favorite destination for rock climbers, who can be seen clinging to the rock like colorful spiders.

The Turtle Rock Loop is suitable for families with young children, and there are four restrooms near the trail.

Majestic views abound at Vedauwoo.

PHOTO BY ANN HUNT

GETTING THERE: From Fort Collins, take U.S. 287 to Laramie, Wyoming, and then take Interstate 80 17 miles southeast to exit 329, the Vedauwoo exit. Drive east on Forest Service Road 700, which is paved, to the campground entrance. There is a fee for day use if you park near the east or west Turtle Rock trailheads in the campground area. If you don't mind a little extra walking, free parking is available about 0.3 mile east on the gravel portion of Forest Service Road 700, past the campground entrance and on the north side of the road. There is also a fee for overnight camping.

THE ROUTE: The trailhead is accessed from a paved parking area about 0.2 mile from the entrance kiosk. You can take the trail west from the lower parking area or go east from the upper parking area—the route described here. Your hike consists of an easy walk around a granite dome, aptly named Turtle Rock.

The trails leads through aspen groves.

PHOTO BY ANN HUNT

At many points along the trail there are interesting rock formations to investigate and enjoy. From the east trailhead, walk through a pine and aspen woodland near the campground road, go through a gate, and continue past a stream running among large boulders. Next, pass a riparian area choked with willows. You will soon gain good views of flat meadows surrounded by the granite spires and pinnacles of the Devils Playground. As you head west, marvel at the large granite formations and the rocks balanced precariously above you. Take note of the beaver dams built in the nearby stream. Follow the path through stands of aspen and proceed through another gate. When you reach the western trailhead, you will quickly realize that you have completed the loop.

TRAILHEAD

N

BOUNDARY

Youngsters in the Woods

Try to recall some of your first hiking experiences. In all likelihood, they were with your family at a time when you were young and lacked the resources to be in the woods on your own.

Positive hiking experiences at an early age, especially within the security of family, can create a sense of self-confidence and a lifelong appreciation for the wonders of our natural world.

If you will be including pre-teen youngsters in your hiking trips, some advance preparation and understood rules can assure a safe and stress-free experience:

- The surest way to avoid a lost-child situation in the woods is to have every child observed by an adult at all times. While this may sometimes seem burdensome, it is the surest way to avoid a problem.

- Provide information—leave a note on your dashboard, readable from the outside of your vehicle, stating how many adults and children are in your party, where you are going, and when you expect to return. This could be valuable information to an emergency team.

- Identify your young companions—equip each young hiker with a note or card describing who they are and who you are, where you live, how you can be reached (by cell phone or otherwise), any allergies the child has, etc.

Before your next hiking adventure, think about putting together a small day pack or fanny pack for your child to carry on every outing. The contents can include a loud whistle, a reflecting mirror, several Day-Glo orange strips, one or two bandages, some hard candies or health bars, and a warm hat. Options could include some crayons and blank paper to color on.

If the child is old enough to learn, practice the following simple safety procedures with him or her just in case the child becomes lost:

- **Stay put.** Show them how to decorate a small tree or a bush with the orange flagging. Emphasize the need to stay close to their new "campsite."

- **Stay warm.** The hat goes on right away and stays on. The space blanket gets opened in a sunny spot and, if there is any wind, held down by a few rocks. Show them how to roll up in the blanket if the weather cools down.

- **Stay busy.** Encourage the child to blow the whistle frequently, and show the child how to catch the sun on the mirror and flash its light around.

A bit of preparation can go a long way to ensure the safety and enjoyment of every hiking adventure.

About the Author

JOHN GASCOYNE began his apprenticeship as a writer and photographer at age eighteen when he joined the U.S. Navy. By age twenty, he was editor of the ship's newspaper aboard a guided missile cruiser. At Colorado State University in Fort Collins, he held several positions on the *CSU Collegian* and served as its editor his senior year. After college, he edited the *Northern Colorado Star,* a bi-weekly commercial newspaper in Fort Collins.

Although some questionable guidance counseling led John to law school, his passion for writing stayed strong. Among other contributions, for two years he wrote a weekly column for the *Fort Collins Coloradoan.* His present passions include working toward a peaceful world and a healthy environment.

The Best Fort Collins Hikes has allowed John to further indulge in his fascination with the written word and his enduring appreciation for nature and the Colorado outdoors.

Checklist

The Best Fort Collins Hikes

☐ Hike 1 American Lakes (or Michigan Lakes) 14

☐ Hike 2 Arthur's Rock 18

☐ Hike 3 Big South 22

☐ Hike 4 Black Powder Trail 26

☐ Hike 5 Chasm Lake 30

☐ Hike 6 Crosier Mountain 34

☐ Hike 7 Devil's Backbone—Wild Loop Trail...... 38

☐ Hike 8 Flattop Mountain and Hallett Peak 42

☑ Hike 9 Greyrock Trail............................... 46

☐ Hike 10 Hewlett Gulch............................... 50

☐ Hike 11 Horsetooth Rock 54

☐ Hike 12 Montgomery Pass (#986)................ 58

☐ Hike 13 Mount Margaret 62

☐ Hike 14 Mount McConnell........................... 66

☐ Hike 15 Pawnee Buttes.............................. 70

☐ Hike 16 Poudre Trail................................. 74

☐ Hike 17 Stormy Peaks Trail to
             Stormy Peaks Pass 78

☐ Hike 18 Trap Park.................................... 82

☐ Hike 19 Twin Crater Lakes 86

☐ Hike 20 Vedauwoo/Turtle Rock Loop............. 90